Modern Love

H.M. Brown

IngramSpark

Copyright © 2024 by H.M. Brown

All rights reserved. No part of this book may be reproduced in any form or by any means, electronic or mechanical, including photocopying and recording, or by any information storage and retrieval system, without permission in writing from the publisher.

ISBN: 979-8-218-42256-1 (Paperback)
ISBN: 979-8-218-42257-8 (eBook)

Front cover image and book designed by Meli and Rose L.L.C.

Manufactured in the United States of America.

Dedication

To the people who are hurting
please know you're not alone.

Table of Contents

Panic 1

Dating 16

First Blooms 29

Desire 34

Crossroads 44

Love? 48

The End? 56

Grief 64

Epilogue 76

MODERN LOVE

Panic

Modern Love

Terror
rips through me,
I have–
a desire.

Those seem dirty
for one unworthy
of love

How dare I
have a need,
request something of you
one so unyielding
you've given me the most precious thing,
the gift of time

yet still
I want more.

How do I say
that I'm scared you'll slip away
like all the others?

Modern Love

Growing
out of fear,
out of too muchness,
leaving no room
shrinking
wanting less
gradually dimming
the self.

Craving
the non-
judgemental, un-
attached silence
of
being alone.

MODERN LOVE

How?
In learning the joys of being alone
do you also
learn to love yourself.

Modern Love

It feels like a desire for control
to want to have you near
to want you close beside me

I've seen it

taint the present
paint the future
cast a pallid light on possibilities
erecting gilded cages to keep the evils of the world
 out
fostering the sins of possession within
creating malice unto itself in ways unimaginable

Specters of the past
wrapping round first blooms
choking possibility
harbingers of suffering

Lingering tokens of grief and loss ungovernable…

Modern Love

Could perhaps the notion,
one can govern one's own fears
come from men afraid of the wild?

We are animals after all
haven't you heard?

Modern Love

I suppose I've grown to see men as the enemy
yes,
we all have choice,
of who to follow
what to believe
that is
unless "truth" has been served to you with a threat
conditioned into your psyche
layered underneath shame and guilt
garnished with the fear of abandonment
with promises of death for dessert

Modern Love

for those who fear nothing
but being forsaken in the wild
bombarded by the possibility of aloneness,
are you so willing
to pay the ferryman's toll for love?
in fear's thrall
is there really such a thing as choice?

Modern Love

predisposed to bouts of terror
that fester in our anger
rash decisions in the name of power
that we sometimes mistake for love

We become manic
in our efforts to make structure out of the chaos of emotion
thinking perhaps
that checklists of proper action can give us the roadmap we desire,
the answer to
what's right–

What is right?

Modern Love

Perhaps in this we must start with
what's wrong?

Is it fair to weaponize one's past hurts
use trauma as a shield
or a defense
bullets and bruises
harsh words
curled fists
long silences and separations

when we've all been hurt

Modern Love

Maybe your pain was worse
even though you've healed and others haven't,
or don't,
for 'lesser' things

I'm sure the scales with which we measure
    suffering aren't balanced the same.
we all assume we're starting at zero
but that's never really the case

my worse
could be your Wednesday

we could layer in resilience
and DNA
in an effort to agree on a system of calibration.

Maybe pain
is just pain
is just uncomfortable
is just insane to think we could judge ourselves
on our capacity to stand in horror

Modern Love

counting the seconds
we can hold our breath
until with spotted vision we collapse

We're all humans with soft skin
and softer hearts.

Modern Love

As for me,
I've grown accustomed to turning my panic attacks
into art.
Especially in the winter months
as I wake
and my chest constricts with grief,
I sit up and grab pencil and paper
turn on white screen
and let the cries of flutes keen
as I let my heart bleed out
in pixels and graphite

In a blank page,
I see evidence of idealized purity
which I cover with reality.

Modern Love

It's always been so striking to me
as we hear the cries of others
how we've all convinced each other
that the other must be more cheerful
more self-assured
more put together
than us.

In my limited experience
we're all children
dressed up in wrinkled skin
fearing loss
fearing judgment
fearing abandonment

All desiring love

Modern Love

It doesn't have to be erotic
just simple presence
stability
surety is enough.

On silver screens it looks like big kisses
contortionists under sheets
grand declarations of adoration;

under the simple blue sky
a hand held
a smile shared
a talk over a meal
is comfort,
is enough

Modern Love

Dating

Modern Love

Something casual.
When did that start meaning
someone I don't have to care about?

In a technological revolution,
just get a vibrator if you want to fuck
it'll save us all some time

if what you're looking for is touch
find a cuddle party
get a dog

it's a shame we're so puritanical
we could all pay for sexual comforts
if we wanted to play at love without feelings

promising we won't get attached
then getting attached,
then in cowardice, running away

Modern Love

Relationships are no better.
An excuse to act upon codependence
to be attached to someone
to have the promise of forever
till death do us part
even if that death is by the hand of a lover

dating profiles a façade
in a quest for a mother or maid
father or protector
guardian or stability

someone to drive the ghosts of past hurts away

Modern Love

I think I'm just looking for someone brave enough
    to give a fuck.
Someone who shows up
with a loving word
my favorite foods
tissues–
and matches and shovels to bury unkind pasts
and hurtful words

someone to see my darkness
and raise me the hollow ravages of their own
    bleeding heart

Modern Love

How do we deem some
yet not others
as worthy.

When you dole out breadcrumbs
of magical, mushy affection
chewed up and spent,
lacking nourishment
as if they were gold nuggets.

And then take them back.

My heart is hungry
but your siren honeymoon phase promises
feed only the souls in hell
with too long a spoon

Modern Love

I like to tie things up
into neat little boxes of certainty
easily identifiable
I'll settle for
the modern labels of love.

Situationship,
relationship,
lover,
cohabitation partner,
ex that never moved out because living alone is so
    god damn expensive.

It creates definition
certainty
clarity in a world
as clear as mud
where promises of forever
mean nothing.

Modern Love

What are we?
whatever you want to be
said in mockery
as life is not always
as we want it to be,

a concept dependent on
wanting the same thing(s).

Of stepping into desire,
the ability
to identify
lust
and need
and want

and compare it against
what is personally
and mutually
beneficial.

Modern Love

I lost the ability to understand
or distinguish between
the labels of modern attachments
two false loves ago.

Modern Love

And what of the labor of love?
do the highs
outweigh the lows?

or is it more to do
with finding someone
who can pick you up and hug you,
or drag you,
through the hardest spots in life
kicking and screaming
until you remember
how pretty the blue skies are
and how good ice cream tastes.

Someone who will witness your rock bottom
your empty
your soul laid bare
and not give up.
What then does that make you?

Modern Love

lovers
accountability buddies
the starcrossed and deluded
partners in determined badassery
the too stubborn to give up?

Modern Love

I could never decide when our anniversary was.

Was it the day we matched
the day we met
the day we were girlfriends
or
one of the many days I decided to stay
instead of running away
(and vice versa).

How do you measure
the passage of time
in a construct?

Modern Love

Perhaps you can mark it
in the number of meltdowns
almost break ups
arguments
goodbyes,
the false and the forever,
the will we ever see each other agains.

The one thing about sad things
is that they add a period
to the end of a bated breath

They offer finality
where happiness seemed so infinite.

Modern Love

In the face of a dreamer's infinity
terror lurks
in the finite reality
of endings promised

Modern Love

First Blooms

Modern Love

I wish I could write of love
as other poets do
with flowery words and metaphors
gentle caresses
fluttering hearts

Modern Love

As a queer it's quite a shame
that I don't wax poetic about soft skin
kind smiling eyes
trembling mounds and apexes–

I suppose those are men's words
desires played out
over centuries of censure

but porn exists,
and I'm too numbed out by heartache
for the gossamer wings in my chest
to mean anything
but panic attacks

Modern Love

My love dreams? inspired by
desires for safety
that my baggage will be checked
at a lovely soul's door
and treated with respect,
always claimed
tagged fragile

I don't want the faint of heart
even if they've cherry lips
I'd rather foreheads well-worn
for staring up at the moon
wondering what terrors the next eclipse will
    bring

one just as quick to cackle at the follies of
    humans
as they are to give a gentle hug
as they are to open their heart in warmth

Modern Love

those simple things will melt my guard
so I can feel the soft oblivion
your kisses bring
as my mind relaxes into pleasure.

Modern Love

Desire

Modern Love

My language of love is company.
I would have made a great [companion],
I can listen for hours
to the tallest of tales
with the kindest of hearts
digging into the darkest enclaves of personhood
craving the site of the core of one's being
tugging on tendrils of terror
through the deepest of repressive woods
hoping to meet the
crashing waves of release
as the walls of shame fall

Most content when people feel heard
but removing every trace of myself from
    conversation

Modern Love

Around others,
I feel numb–
never trusting,
waiting for the hurt
after knowing what it is to love

Staying present
while feeling cavernous
boundaries guard my heart
my mind adrift in other things

Modern Love

The way another's soul alights
when they feel seen,
understood,
is the most curious thing.

Perhaps it's universal
for others to get off on feeling captivating;

or perhaps it's just the souls I meet

once comfortable,
we all desire attention
so that
for even a moment
self-doubt can go fuck itself
for there is proof
that you matter
that someone else cares

Modern Love

It is a game to some,
the devilish twinkle in their eye
as they alight on prey.

Feathers splayed
they prance about
in seductive displays of bravado

like hunting
or snake charming
seeing how close you can get
undetected or mesmerizing
without spooking your target

Fancy garb
wondrous scents
delights of taste and touch
teasing until you reach an edge
then pounce

Modern Love

eyes open,
you linger...
will they fly when released
or lean in

Modern Love

From there
the long game of opportunities,
not a trap set to spring
but breadcrumbs lain in different directions

more than sweaty bodies
more than basic consent
it is a dance
along a winding path
that dips and sways
until two (or more) are heavy with need
and you collapse onto each other with abandon

Modern Love

but even then,
you still tease
building
and nipping
to an ecstatic yes–
misplaced parts and laughter
as you ease into knowing each other

testing tongues in places
asking for directions to the best spots to eat
nibbling the nectars of sweat
and sweet
and sour
and salty

the spectrum of taste that is arousal
a sumptuous feast for the hungry

Modern Love

it's playful kisses
pleasure returned
the humble reverence of discovery

the knowledge that no two forms are the same
regardless of anatomy

it's listening to the catch in breath
feeling squirms of pleasure
anticipating sensitive spots,
being wrong
being redirected
bodies angled for comfort
and reciprocal play
even when you're the focus

Modern Love

it's laughter
because sex is silly
sensual
a surreptitious sensory scape of gluttony
gorgeous and good
even without orgasms

delightfully delicious
to desire to play
with the dips and curves
of another
within the confines of consent

the recognition that permission is sexy
Per a mutually agreed upon mission
to coax pleasure
out of desire

MODERN LOVE

Crossroads

Modern Love

Inevitably
we all find ourselves at a fork.

Do we pursue pleasure,
comfort,
familiar toxins,
company,
cultured purity,
or something else.

Modern Love

From here,
relationships survive
they thrive
or burn out
and die
the Darwinian Tale of competition

MODERN LOVE

We are left to consider,
did our dance of seduction land
or was it a few beats out of step?

with cards laid out on table,
what will our next move be?

MODERN LOVE

Love?

Modern Love

I wasn't sure what to put here.

Modern Love

Everything I know of love
is quite complex
for a word, of only four letters,
it holds so much nuance
and edge

Love is loving
through pain
through disappointment
through grief
through loss
through endings
and never talk to me agains
through forced goodbyes
and safety plans

Modern Love

It's a reminder that even when love is for someone
    else
you must come first
for you cannot love
if you are dead

It's the desire to protect something else
not for its use
but because it is precious

Modern Love

Liberation
of expectations
of terms
of conditions

Disagreements and distance
with determination to send someone off
with the reminder that
this life,
is their own
to do
and make of it what they will

that one's distaste means nothing
in the face of the wide-eyed dream
of the one you love

Modern Love

Even if
in your hands
my heart breaks,
I'll never be
whole
the same way
again.

Modern Love

Your miser's hands,
one
grasps on to
illusory affection
the other
reaching out
demanding payment
before relinquishing
counterfeit love.

My body cleaves to you
in all ways–
grasping
gasping
desperate,
painfully split in two

Modern Love

What do you do?
Pay a soul's price
for false affection

Or cobble together
the scattered pieces
of the suddenly shattered
you

Modern Love

The End?

Modern Love

The recognition of two paths meeting,
converging,
and eventually splitting
as all things have a natural end

yes,

even within the infinity of love
two embers still, eventually, burn out
to one day become the charcoal of another flame
to ashes
to fertilizer
for new lands
of volcanic possibility

Modern Love

We forget perhaps
that when we fall
we must crash
and burst
into a thousand pieces.

Modern Love

I lay in bed
for hours
unhinged.

Wondering,
what I did wrong
if it was my fault
if I could have been better

Looked better
smiled better
laughed better
loved better

What could I have done, better.

Modern Love

At the end,
in this vacant space
my ears,
ring with grief
as the light goes out
the stupid bit of hope I allowed to slip in,
leaves.

I should have known.

Nothing is forever in this snowflake world.

Everything is conditional
fleeting
merely temporary.

Modern Love

My chest aches for loving you.
It is said
that there is no bigger strength
than loving with your whole heart
so completely.

It is folly.

The strength comes
from scraping pieces of yourself
off the floor
in the shameful quiet moments
of wondering
how being alive can hurt so much
in fantasizing
of death

Modern Love

Our end shouldn't mean mine

At the very least
I'll live for art
for the chance to give back
for the words to flow from my aching chest
through my fingers
into the world on paper
to perhaps
one day
find someone else who is grieving
to show them they are not alone
to verify for them
that love is not always beautiful
sometimes it sucks–
it hurts so bad,
it feels like the most stupid thing to fall for

But fall for it again you might
you probably will

Modern Love

For after every ending
after all grief
after the panic
the dastardly seed of love
may still bloom again.

Modern Love

Grief

Modern Love

This tale
I know well.

In a collection
of the tales of modern love
it's quite bizarre that
of all the parts
I know grief the best

Modern Love

It seems I've said goodbye a thousand times
in a lifetime that's so short
shorter still than the oldest person
even more minute than the universe
and just as quick is lost

One moment there
the next gone
like magic

Modern Love

The grandest trick of all
performed by mere mortals
the magically untrained
to disappear forever.
A spirit slipped away
leaving behind a quickly decaying meat suit
for organisms to feed on
and regenerate

Modern Love

In that light,
one would think breakups are easier
while in death
goodbye is not a choice

to consciously uncouple is complex
for two whose souls have danced
it is goodbye
knowing that the other lives on
just without you

it can feel like a waste
that perfectly good love
a comfortable situation
must end

and for what!
to find your way,
blindly
in the cold
darkness
of independence
once your heart has found a home

Modern Love

in the warmth of
company

Modern Love

Some people want more perhaps than surety
that someone else is there to help with bills
that someone else will notice if you choke
that someone will visit you if you're ill

maybe I am too young to think on such things
as money, company, and comfort

Or maybe that's just what this is
the desire for a soul
who will stick around
to laugh at pain with you
so you don't have to cry alone

Modern Love

The empty spaces catch
a fresh cut
never allowed to rest and repair,
in the daily motions of life
an accidental hit
and a river of red springs forth
once again
from a wound that had almost closed

Maddening emptiness

Anderson[1] said that "grief is love
with nowhere to go"
so it spills out
in wails
and salty tears
as the elements do
until they find a container
to build up in
until disturbed once again

---

1 Quote by Jamie Anderson.

Modern Love

In the vacant space
I am numb.

It is empty
cold winds blow here
it is inhospitable
so I neither eat
nor sleep
nor drink

I lay to die
not finding death
not finding peace

Curled into myself
I weep
for the loss is too much

Modern Love

The cycle of healing
and breaking

some say you grow stronger
some believe more fragile
some who like broken things,
believe you become more beautiful

I don't know–
I suppose you just become different.

never the same as before knowing
never the same again
and after again being broken,
your next self will be different still

Modern Love

In all the tears I've shed for love lost,
new love always brings fear
for I do not love by halves

even on my enemies,
I do not wish this pain,
if only one could change
in a rose-colored way
become more empathetic
learn the error of their ways
there are so many hurt souls
stumbling around hurting other souls
drunkards driving through love
even for them, I wish all the best
and what they deserve.

And so I am terrified
of starting again
but know that I can
that in my loneliness I will
that in my disgust I still have compassion
for all the soft souls out there.

Modern Love

I just know that I'll be different
not braver, not stronger, just different
like a snake
shedding a layer
that no longer serves it

then I'll eat it
the pain
the loss
the hurt
like a jagged little pill
to always remember
the path behind just burned
the path ahead on fire

Yet one day
I'll be ready again
to start anew.

MODERN LOVE

Epilogue

Modern Love

There is an alternate ending
to the cycle of modern love.

Modern Love

The backup ending
as old as time
as memory

the illusive,
contentment.

The selfish I
of selfless healing
the inner distillation
of past panic and grief

Modern Love

Bandaging bruises
before dipping toes
into the depths of another.

Finally
holding space
for the ugly faces
of inner longings
untended and starved
out of shame.

Becoming beautiful
as self defined
with audacity

Modern Love

The
I dare
have a need.
Occupying spaces
with unyielding requests
of the most precious thing,
time.

I make them of myself.
The time to sit
with dirty secrets
the unworthiness
the hurt
the fear of love.

Contemplating the double-edged tragedy
that is desire
under the expansive depth of night.
The time where yearning
can find stillness
as it has space to breathe
underneath the stars.

MODERN LOVE

Growing
out of love
out of healing,
leaving no room
for shrinking
wanting less
finding contentment in
the self.

Rooting into space(s).

Still craving
the non-
judgemental, un-
attached silence—
but now of
self-acceptance.

Modern Love

I wonder what
modern love would be like
if we held space
for self-
empathy

time for
collective healing

compassion for
shame and mistakes made

and a dose of humility
for forgiveness?

About the Author

H.M. Brown is an artist, poet, and writer. The owner of Meli and Rose, an art shop where a portion of the proceeds of every art piece and art print sold are donated to a cause.

H publishes poems regularly on Caia Rose Blog and writes on Medium.

Follow H on:
caiaroseblog.com
meliandrose.com

Milton Keynes UK
Ingram Content Group UK Ltd.
UKHW021221050724
445102UK00015B/325